Contents

About Australia

The **continent** of Australia is a huge **island**. It is surrounded by the Indian Ocean and the Pacific Ocean. More than 8,000 small islands are in the oceans surrounding Australia. Australia is the smallest of Earth's seven continents.

PACIFIC OCEAN

continent one of Earth's seven large land masses

island piece of land that is surrounded by water

by Christine Juarez

First Facts®

Raintree is an imprint of Capstone Global Library Limited, a company incorporated in England and Wales having its registered office at 264 Banbury Road, Oxford, OX2 7DY – Registered company number: 6695582

www.raintree.co.uk
myorders@raintree.co.uk

Designed by Cynthia Della-Rovere and Clare Webber
Picture research by Svetlana Zhurkin
Production by Kathy McColley
Originated by Capstone Global Library Ltd
Printed and bound in India

ISBN 978 1 4747 6111 6 (hardcover)
22 21 20 19 18
10 9 8 7 6 5 4 3 2 1

ISBN 978 1 4747 6117 8 (paperback)
23 22 21 20 19
10 9 8 7 6 5 4 3 2 1

British Library Cataloguing in Publication Data
A full catalogue record for this book is available from the British Library.

Acknowledgements
We would like to thank the following for permission to reproduce photographs:
Capstone Global Library Ltd, 5, 9; Dreamstime: Rozenn Leard, 19; iStockphoto: FiledImage, 9 (inset); Shutterstock: Debra James, 15 (back), FocusDzign, 21, Holli, 16, Hypervision Creative, 11, Ian Crocker, cover (top), Jeremy Red, 8, Petar B photography, 13, pierdest, 7, Przemyslaw Reinfus (pattern), cover (left) and throughout, psirob, 17, robert cicchetti, 15 (inset), Taras Vyshnya, cover (middle), Viacheslav Rashevskyi, cover (bottom right), back cover, 1, 3, worldswildlifewonders, cover (bottom left)

ARCTIC OCEAN

CONTINENTS OF THE WORLD

NORTH
AMERICA

EUROPE

ASIA

ATLANTIC
OCEAN

AFRICA

PACIFIC
OCEAN

EQUATOR

SOUTH
AMERICA

INDIAN
OCEAN

AUSTRALIA

SOUTHERN OCEAN

ANTARCTICA

Famous places

Australia is home to many famous places. Some are **modern**. The Sydney Opera House opened in 1973. Its roof looks like the sails of a ship.

Some well-known places are natural landmarks. Uluru is a giant hill of red rock in central Australia. It is an important place for the Aboriginal people. It has many caves and **ancient** rock paintings.

modern up-to-date or new in style
ancient from a long time ago

Uluru is also called Ayers Rock.

Geography

Huge, dry deserts cover much of western and central Australia. The biggest is the Great Victoria Desert. It is known for its red sand **dunes**.

On the eastern side of Australia is a long line of mountains. It is called the Great Dividing Range. Mount Kosciuszko is to the south. It is Australia's highest mountain.

Fact: Mount Kosciuszko is 2,228 metres (7,310 feet) tall.

dune hill or ridge of sand piled up by the wind

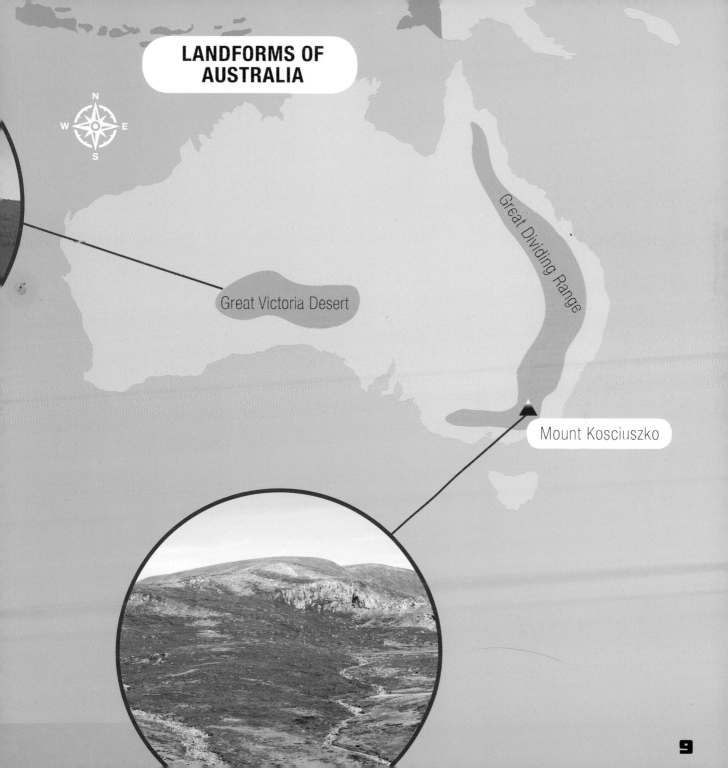

LANDFORMS OF AUSTRALIA

Great Victoria Desert

Great Dividing Range

Mount Kosciuszko

The Murray and Darling rivers meet to make the Murray-Darling River. It is Australia's longest river at 3,824 kilometres (2,376 miles).

Lake Eyre is the biggest lake in Australia. It is a salt lake. In the last 100 years, the lake has only completely filled with water three times.

Murray-Darling River

Weather

Most of Australia has hot, dry weather. Wildfires can spread across the land when it is very dry. Australia's far northern and eastern parts have warm weather with lots of rain.

Australia is in the Southern Hemisphere. It has opposite seasons to the Northern Hemisphere. Winter lasts from June to September. Summer lasts from December to March.

Fact: Snow falls only high in the Australian Alps. These mountains are in southeastern Australia.

A thunderstorm brings rain to southeastern Australia.

Animals

Australia is home to unique wildlife. Koalas and kangaroos are found only in Australia. These animals carry their young in pouches. The Great Barrier Reef runs along the northeast coast of Australia. It is the biggest **coral reef** in the world. It is home to an amazing number of animals. The reef includes 1,500 types of fish.

Great Barrier Reef

coral reef type of land made up of the hardened bodies of corals; corals are small, colourful sea creatures

koalas

Plants

Eucalyptus trees grow all over Australia. Their leaves make an oil that has a strong smell. Koalas eat the leaves. They eat so many leaves their fur smells like the plant.

One unusual type of plant grows in the desert. It is called the Sturt's desert pea. It is covered in bright red and black flowers.

Sturt's desert pea

eucalyptus tree

People

About 24 million people live in Australia. Australia is both a country and a continent. Canberra is the capital. Sydney is the biggest city.

The Aboriginals were the first people to live in Australia. They came from Southeast Asia around 60,000 years ago. Today many Aboriginals live in cities and towns, as well as in the countryside, in Australia.

A family wears traditional Aboriginal clothing and paint. The man is playing an instrument called a didgeridoo.

Natural resources and products

Australia has many **natural resources**. Much of the land is used for farming. Farmers keep sheep on large farms in the dry outback. The sheep are mainly raised for their wool.

Gold, iron ore and other metals are mined in Australia. There are also huge diamond mines. Most of the world's opals come from Australia. The continent also has oil, gas and coal.

natural resource material from nature that is useful to people

sheep on an Australian farm

Glossary

ancient from a long time ago

continent one of Earth's seven large land masses

coral reef type of land made up of the hardened bodies of corals; corals are small, colourful sea creatures

dune hill or ridge of sand piled up by the wind

island piece of land that is surrounded by water

modern up-to-date or new in style

natural resource material from nature that is useful to people

Find out more

Books

Australia (Mathalon Maps), Joanne Randolph (Raintree, 2017)

Australia (My Holiday in...), Jane Bingham (Wayland, 2014)

This is Australia, Kevin Pettman (Wayland, 2018)

Websites

www.dkfindout.com/uk/earth/continents/australasia-and-oceania/

Learn more about Australia including its wildlife, habitats and landmarks.

www.natgeokids.com/uk/discover/geography/countries/facts-about-australia/

Discover fascinating facts about Australia, including information on its 36 species of poisonous spiders and 20 species of venomous snakes!

Comprehension questions

1. What is Uluru? What group of people is it important to?

2. The koala is an animal that lives only in Australia. Describe the koala and what it eats.

3. When does winter occur in Australia? When does summer occur?

Index